Copyright © 2021

All rights reserved.
No part of this publication, or the characters within it, may be reproduced or distributed in any form or by any means without prior written consent from the publisher.

Written by
Sandrian Nelson-Moon

Illustrations by
Bex Sutton

First Edition 2021

This Book Belongs To:

....

....

Itty Bitty Betty
& The Cookies

By Sandrian Nelson - Moon

Illustrated By Bex Sutton

Itty Bitty Betty was small as can be,
About as tall as her mom's knee!
After a fun day out by the sea...

Itty Bitty wanted cookies for tea!

Looking around the kitchen door,
She tiptoed across the shiny floor.

"No cookies here," she said in a pity,
And recruited the help of her brown kitty.
"I need a ladder!" exclaimed Itty Bitty.
"To find the best cookies in the city.

Pulling the ladder with a heave ho,
She climbed up the ladder really slow,
Spotting the cookies with a delighted, "whoa!"
She reached out to grab them on a tip toe.

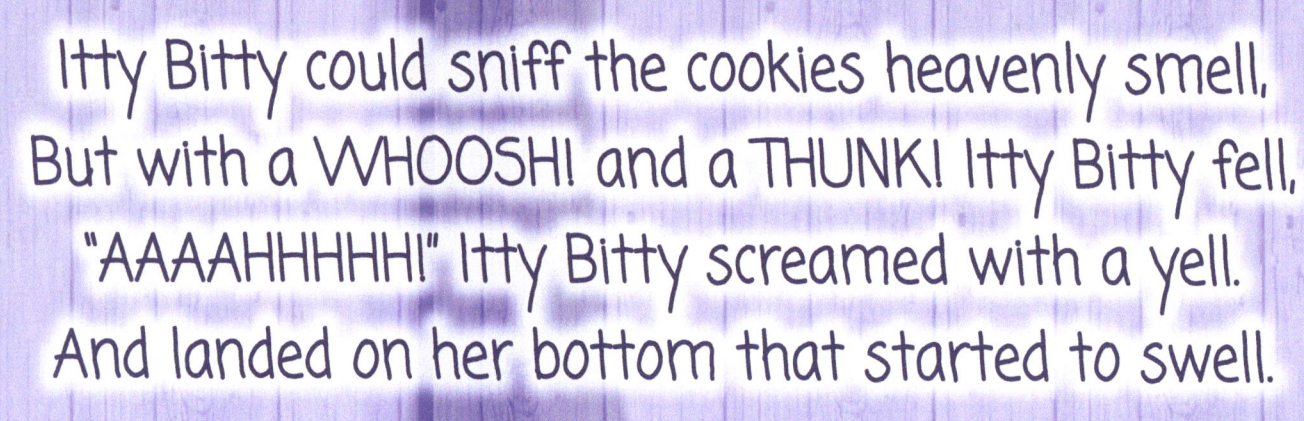

Itty Bitty could sniff the cookies heavenly smell,
But with a WHOOSH! and a THUNK! Itty Bitty fell,
"AAAAHHHHH!" Itty Bitty screamed with a yell.
And landed on her bottom that started to swell.

Itty Bitty rubbed her bum with a sigh,
And decided to give it another try.
She stood and climbed the steps up high.
Picturing those cookies in her mind's eye.

Moving up the ladder at a slow crawl,
She looked down and saw she was up so tall,
Stretching her arms out that were so small,
She gulped as she tried not to fall.

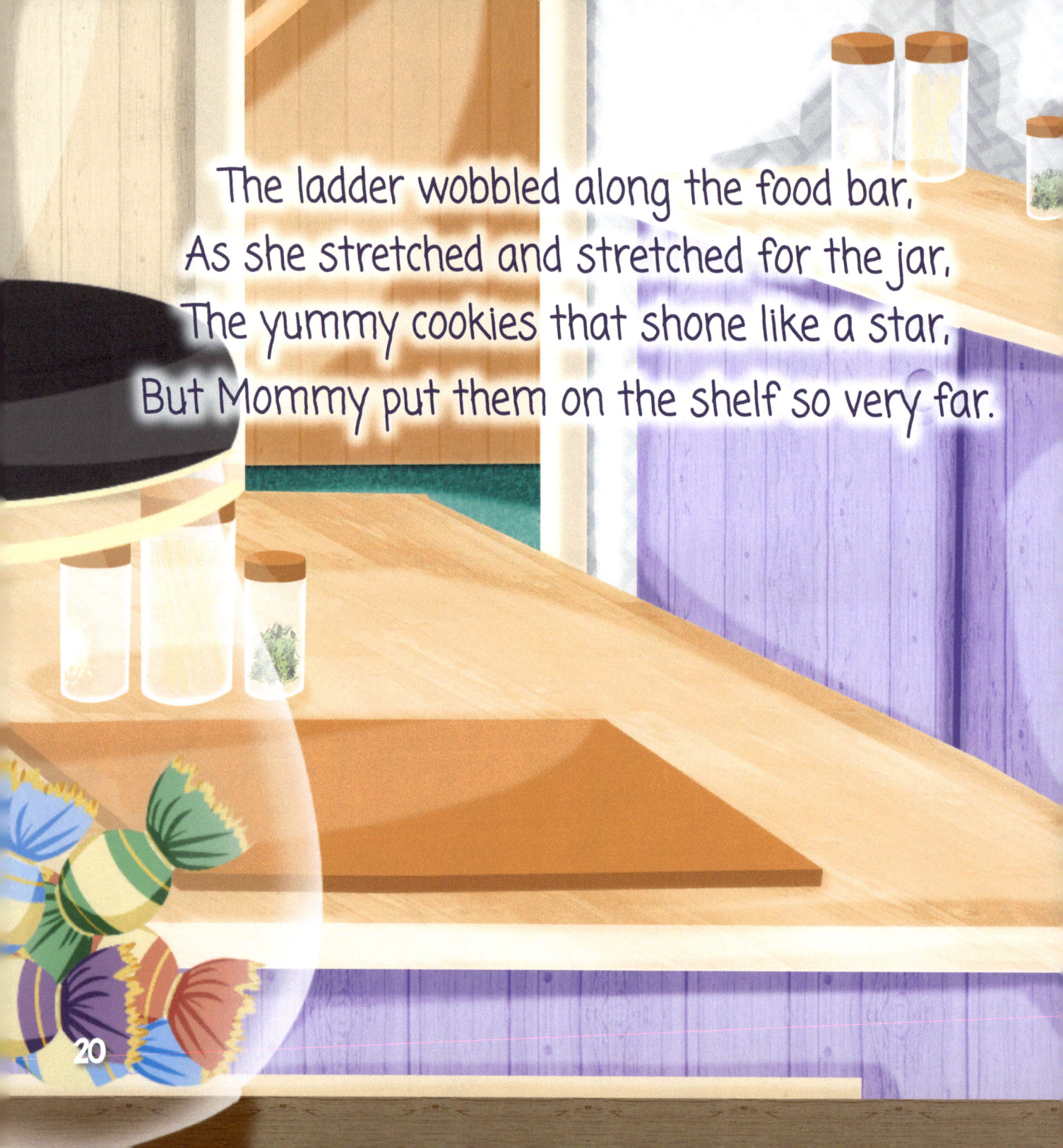

The ladder wobbled along the food bar,
As she stretched and stretched for the jar,
The yummy cookies that shone like a star,
But Mommy put them on the shelf so very far.

Closer...

Closer...

Closer...

"FREEZE!"

Mommy shouted as Itty Bitty stood still as trees.

When she wobbled Mommy picked her up with ease,
And hugged her tight until she started to wheeze.

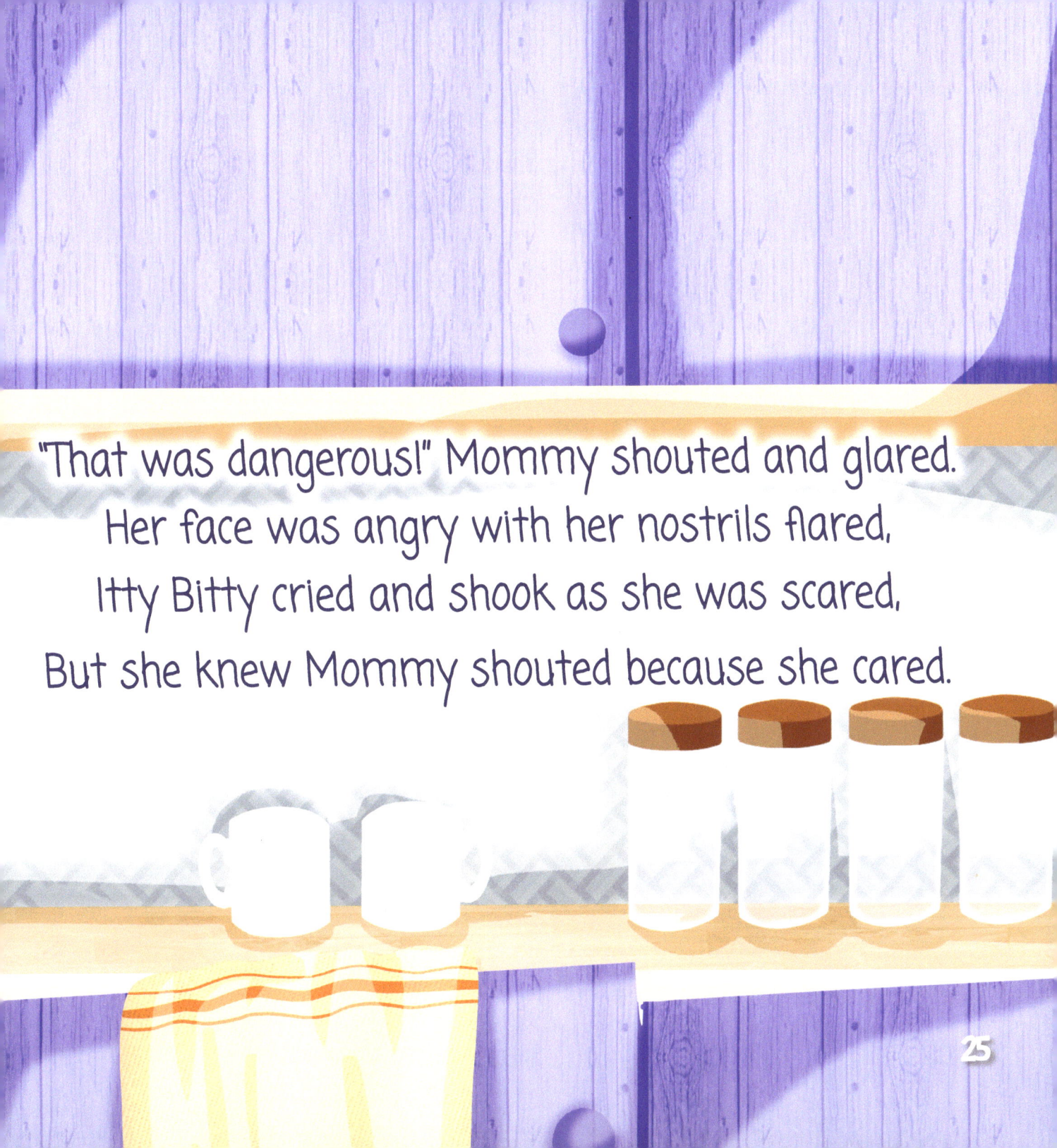

"That was dangerous!" Mommy shouted and glared.
Her face was angry with her nostrils flared,
Itty Bitty cried and shook as she was scared,
But she knew Mommy shouted because she cared.

"I'm sorry," Itty Bitty cried with a big hug,
"I just wanted a special cookie from the jug."
Mummy pulled her towards her with a tug,
And wrapped her in her arms until she was snug.

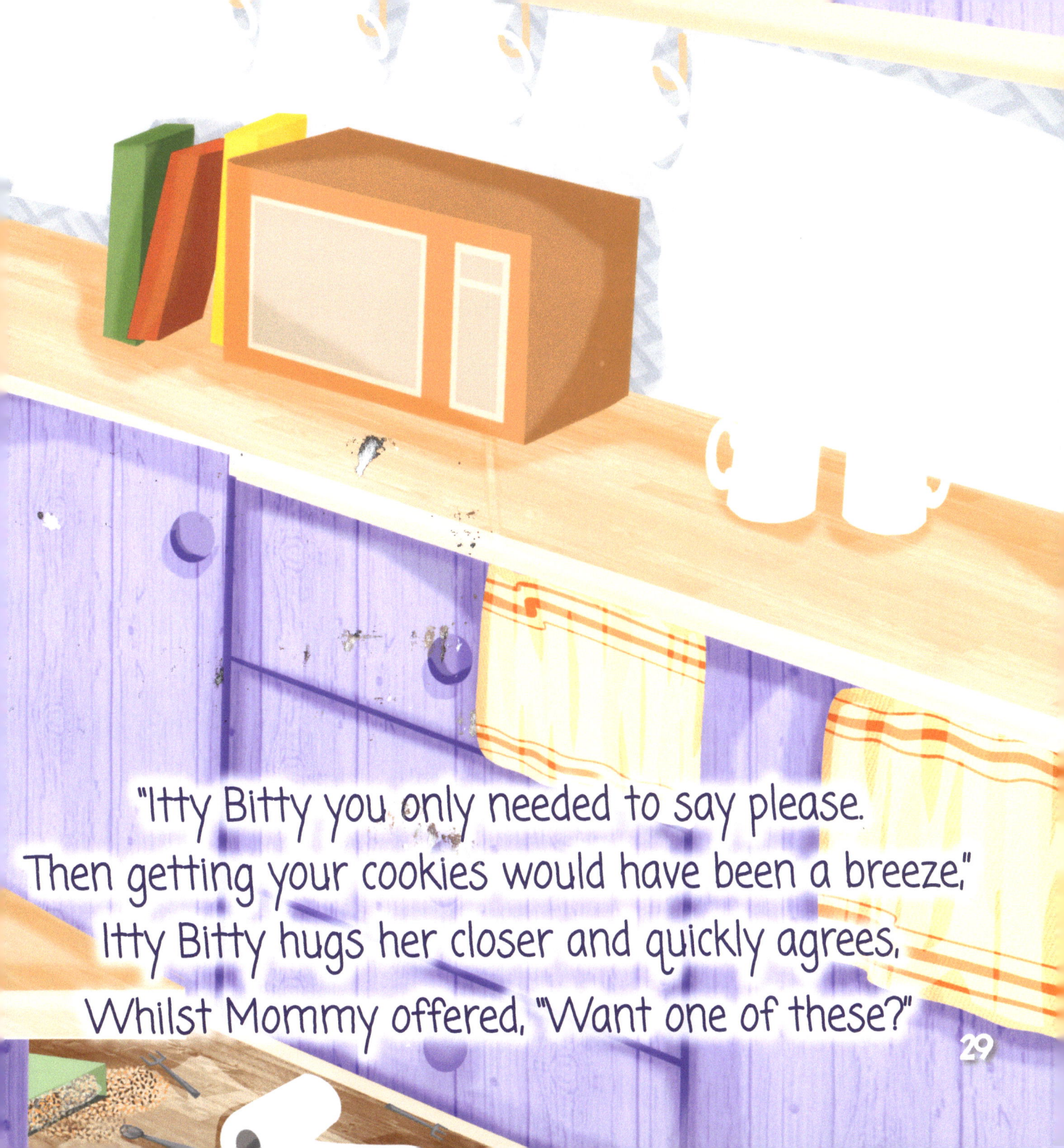

"Itty Bitty you only needed to say please.
Then getting your cookies would have been a breeze,"
Itty Bitty hugs her closer and quickly agrees,
Whilst Mommy offered, "Want one of these?"

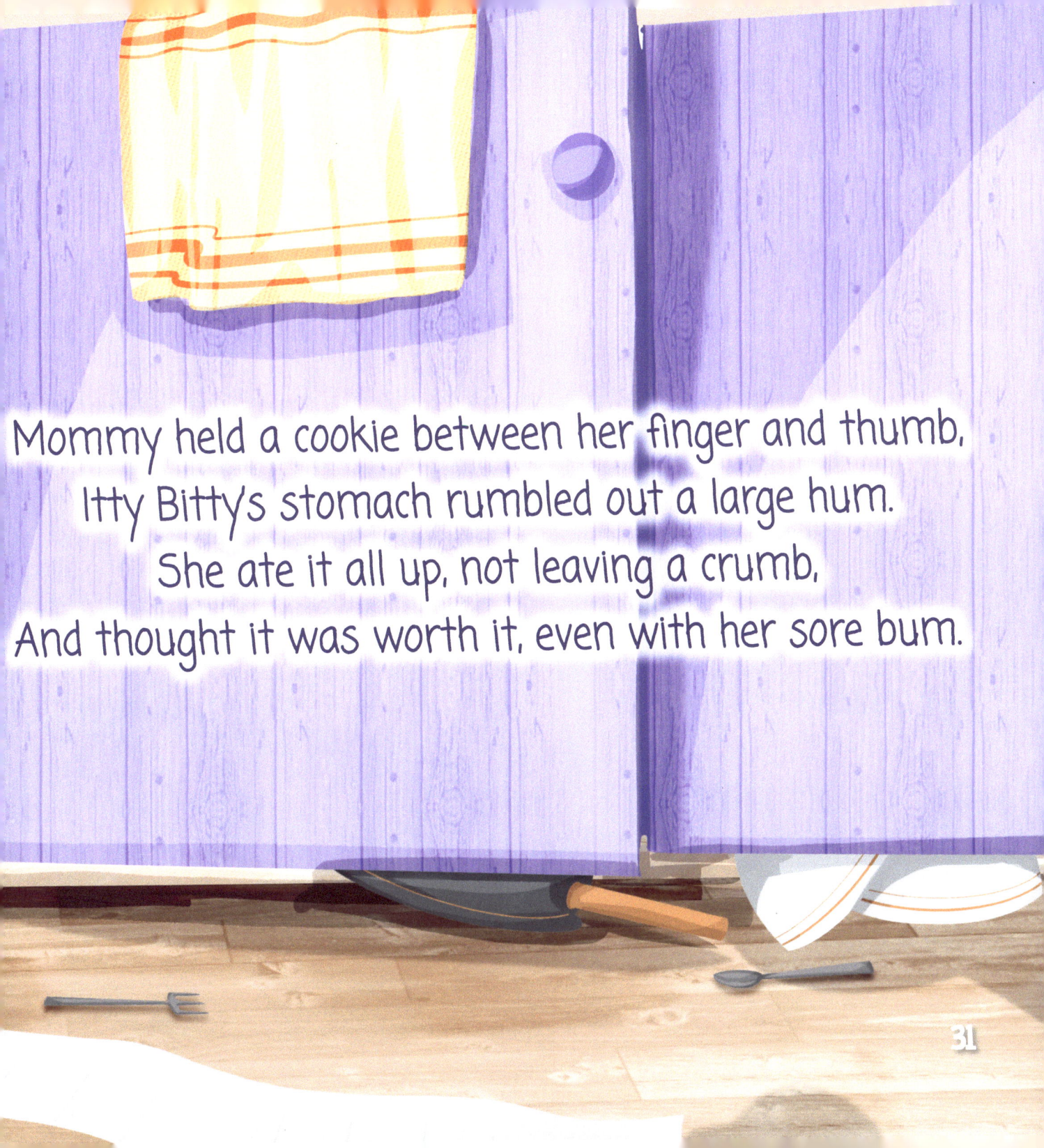

Mommy held a cookie between her finger and thumb,
Itty Bitty's stomach rumbled out a large hum.
She ate it all up, not leaving a crumb,
And thought it was worth it, even with her sore bum.

About The Author

Sandrian Nelson-Moon is a humble example of perseverance and faith and believes a child's imagination and education is their fuel to true development.

Sandrian is a wife, mom, entrepreneur, Queens County Committee Member by day, future attorney, and novelist by night. Sandrian advocates strongly for children, victims of sexual and personal trauma, and has won numerous awards for community service.

A Jamaican native, she is a lover of seafood, family time, travel, and beaches. Currently residing in a borough she loves, you'll find her most likely multitasking.

She can be reached by email at sandriannmoon@gmail.com

CPSIA information can be obtained
at www.ICGtesting.com
Printed in the USA
BVHW051511220421
605631BV00002B/36